THE THINKING KID'S GUIDE TO SUCCESSFUL

SOCCER

NINA SAVIN SCOTT

illustrations by ANNE CANEVARI GREEN

The Millbrook Press
Brookfield, Connecticut

Dedicated to Bill Scott, a tremendous soccer coach.

Special thanks to Nate and Tess and their soccer teammates, and Haley on the sidelines; and the coaches and athletes of the boys' varsity soccer teams of Phillips Academy (1987–1997) and Suffield Academy (1980–1987), and the men's and women's varsity soccer teams of Stanford University (1997). Thanks, too, to the wonderful Pete and Elaine Savin and clans Clark, Scott and Sullivan, the Drs. Vale, Dean Conway, Craig Tornberg, Cathy Gregory Gannes, Lucy Bowen Sykes, Bud Graham and Phillips Academy (for the opportunity), Jean Reynolds (for everything), and Major League Soccer.

Library of Congress Cataloging-in-Publication Data
Scott, Nina Savin.
The thinking kid's guide to successful soccer / Nina Savin Scott ; illustrations by Anne Canevari Green.
p.   cm.
Includes bibliographical references (p.   ) and index.
Summary: Presents strategies for playing soccer under pressure, dealing with various situations during a game, setting goals, playing with teammates, coping with coaches, and dealing with doubts and fears.
ISBN 0-7613-0324-3 (lib. bdg.)
1. Soccer for children—Juvenile literature. 2. Soccer—Psychological aspects—Juvenile literature. [1. Soccer.] I. Green, Anne Canevari. II. Title.
GV944.2.S36   1999
796.344'2—dc21   98-17201   CIP   AC

Published by The Millbrook Press, Inc.
2 Old New Milford Road
Brookfield, Connecticut 06804

CONTENTS

INTRODUCTION

A man named W. Timothy Gallwey wrote a book in 1974, before all of you were born, called *The Inner Game of Tennis*. It was a revolutionary book at the time, because it wasn't about a tennis player's game against an opponent on the other side of the net. Instead, it was about a tennis player's "inner game."

"This is the game that takes place in the mind of the player," Gallwey wrote, "and it is played against such obstacles as lapses in concentration, nervousness, self-doubt, and self-condemnation."[1]

Gallwey wrote that athletes who play their inner game well—in other words, who develop the best mental attitude—get the most satisfaction from playing their sport. They also play their best, and so give themselves the best opportunity to win.

These days, it is not at all unusual to find sports books that deal with the inner—or mental—side of an athlete's game. What was once considered revolutionary is now universally accepted as true: An athlete's thoughts and feelings matter enormously and have an impact not only on performance but on the athlete's happiness.

Most sports psychology books were written for adults who think very differently than kids do. Yet research on the psychology of youth sports shows that, fundamentally, what's true for adults is true for kids, too: Your success as an athlete is profoundly affected by your thoughts and feelings.

In order to be the best soccer player you can be, you need to spend a lot of time kicking around a soccer ball. But you also need to *think* about the game and your role in it, and that's where this book comes in. It will help you sort out your thoughts and feelings, so you can make the most of your soccer experience.

It doesn't matter if you are already a skilled player or if you're just beginning this sport. It doesn't matter if you are a talented athlete or not. Each one of you is a soccer player with inner thoughts and feelings that matter. You deserve the joy of playing soccer all your life, and the chance to play it as well as you possibly can. The whole world's waiting for you. Join the game.

CHAPTER 1

GET IN THE ZONE

When Joe-Max Moore was twelve years old, he knew he wanted to be a professional soccer player. He didn't know it in a casual way, the way young people think they know they want to be a doctor or an actor or a spy. He knew it seriously and deeply, and he was determined that it would become true.

So, he played soccer all the time. His parents tried to drag him home after his games, and they tried to haul him in for dinner, but he just asked politely if they'd mind waiting a couple of hours, because he wasn't finished practicing his soccer.

Joe-Max Moore was a star in high school and at UCLA and now plays midfield for Major League Soccer's New England Revolution and for the

U.S. Men's National Team. He is only 5 feet 9 inches (175 centimeters) tall, and he weighs 150 pounds (68 kilograms), but if you get anywhere near him when he is playing or even talking about soccer, you can easily understand how he succeeds in elite soccer competition. He is intense.

There's no question that Joe-Max became the best soccer player he could be, and here is how he did it. He loved to play. He loved to practice. He loved to learn and improve. And if he didn't learn a skill right away, or he didn't play well in a game, or he had a problem with a teammate or a coach, he didn't quit the sport. He kept practicing and improving, and when the time was right, he worked the problem out. No one had to tell him to pursue the game he loved.

This is the way that you, too, will become your best at soccer—by playing and practicing the game you love, because you want to do it. No one can make you become your best except you.

Now, most of the time, you'll play your very best soccer when you are having the most fun, rather than when it's most important for you to play well, and here's why. When you are just having fun, your body is relaxed and your mind is completely absorbed in the action.

When you want to play well, however—and especially if you want to play well because you want to win the game—you feel pressure. You put the pressure on yourself, usually, or you feel it from coaches or parents or teammates; in any event, the pressure is on, and it changes things. You aren't as relaxed anymore, and your mind isn't entirely focused on the action, and your performance suffers.

It really isn't fair that the more you care about how well you play, the less chance you have of playing well, but there you have it. What a paradox! Still, it's a paradox you can solve. You can learn to play your best soccer even when you're feeling pressure to perform by learning what it means to get "into the zone."

Getting in the Zone

Let's look very carefully at what happens when you're playing soccer just for fun. Take a game during recess at school, for example. You go from a complete standstill in the school doorway to a full-tilt, rip-snorting, explosive soccer contest in about three seconds flat. You play all out, shouting and sweating and charging the ball; you play confidently and happily. It doesn't matter if you make a mistake; it doesn't even matter if your team loses. In ten minutes, after all, you'll be back at your desk, and the party will be over. The outcome of the game and how well you play are far less important than the playing itself. All you want to do is experience the game while you can.

And you experience each moment fully. If you want to dribble, you dribble. If you want to shoot, you shoot. If you want to go wild and take a risk on a bicycle kick, up you go to try it. So what if you whiff? Your friends won't judge you, because they have no reason to, and even if they did, you wouldn't care.

What's even more important is that you don't judge *yourself*. It doesn't even occur to you to do so. You are so busy having fun you couldn't possibly be bothered with measuring how well you are playing. Since you don't judge yourself, you don't even think about whether you will fail.

When you play soccer this way, you are a state of absorption that's come to be called "the zone." Some athletes call it "flow." You probably don't have a name for it, but you know it when you're there.

The zone doesn't happen only in athletics. It happens when you're dancing or painting or cooking or even, yes, performing a challenging science experiment; it happens whenever you are so interested in what you're doing that you forget about yourself and everything else and just relax your entire body and mind into the activity itself.

Now, when you are playing soccer, the zone is the place you want to be. Lots and lots of books have been written to help people take themselves there. That's because when you're in the zone, you're able to think but your mind isn't crowded with thoughts. You play hard, but it feels easy. Your mind and body work together; everything clicks. And you play your very best.

The Pressure of Competition

It's one thing to get in the zone during those pickup games with your friends. But it's quite another thing to get into the zone when you're playing for your real team in a competitive situation. Lots of time and effort has gone into the arrangements for your game; there are uniforms and schedules and car pools involved; you have a coach and teammates to work with; your parents may be on the sidelines. Most importantly, you are involved in a competitive situation. You are still playing for the purpose of experiencing a soccer game, but your team has a goal: to win the contest. You cannot help but feel pressure to perform.

And when you feel pressure, your mind becomes busy. You think about how well you want to play, and how much you want to win. You think about the people on the sidelines, your coach's expectations, your parents' hopes. You think about how bad it would be if you made a huge mistake, or how sad you'd be if you lost the game.

When the action begins, you keep right on thinking, and the more you want to play well, the more it matters if you don't. Automatically, your thinking turns into worrying.

"I hope I don't blow this shot with everybody watching," you think when you are standing at the penalty line.

"I stink at this sport; I'm just no good," you say to yourself when you boink the ball out of bounds.

"Now our team is losing, and there goes our chance for the tournament," you say when your team is scored on, and so on and so forth, as if you have a little radio embedded in your brain, and it's tuned to a really bad station.

When you think these thoughts, you lose your mental focus, and your body becomes tense. You're no longer in the zone, and you stop playing your best.

Dr. Colleen Hacker, the sports psychologist for the U.S. Women's National Team, says that all competitive athletes have thoughts and images going on in their heads when they play, and 70 percent of the time, the thoughts and images are negative. The only difference between Dr. Hacker's team and yours is that her elite athletes are trained to control those thoughts and images, while you and your teammates probably just suffer the terrible music.

But you can learn to control the thoughts and images in your head. It just takes a little know-how, a little willpower, and a whole, whole lot of practice.

CHAPTER 2

PLAYING WELL UNDER PRESSURE

First of all, if you want to get into the zone during a competitive soccer game, you must understand that it doesn't do you any good to listen to those bad songs on that little radio in your mind. The self-doubt, the worries, the preoccupation with the score—none of these things help you play your best soccer.

Unfortunately, you may believe that you *should* be worrying about how well you play and whether your team is winning. You may think that if you don't worry, you are not trying your hardest or putting forth a maximum effort.

You may even think that it's just not right to go out there in a real game, worry free, and have yourself a grand old time.

But the fact is, you *do* play your best when you're having a grand old time. You *do* play your best when you are not worrying about how well you play or about the score. You need to trust that this is the truth, and allow yourself to dial that radio to a better station.

When Methembe Ndlovu graduated from Dartmouth College in the spring of 1997, having played four years of varsity soccer (and having been chosen to the All-Ivy team three times), he decided to try out for a position on Major League Soccer's San Jose Clash. For three days in August, he joined the Clash during their practice sessions, so the coaches could evaluate his skill. The first two days, Methembe did not want to make any mistakes, so he played carefully, hoping to impress the coaches. The situation was important and stressful, and he responded by thinking a lot about what he should be doing, and whether he was doing it well. In his head, that radio played static. He didn't play his best.

On the third day of the tryout, Methembe finally gave up all hope of making the team. He is a tremendous soccer player, one of the best in the country, but just not quite good enough to play in the premier league, and he knew this. He finally allowed himself to dial up a great song on his mental radio. He knew it wouldn't matter if he made mistakes, so he went ahead and played freely without worrying. He had himself a grand old time. And naturally, he played like a star.

"I figured I had nothing to lose," he said. "So I played my heart out. And yes, I finally played my best. I didn't make the team, but I'll try again some day."

Methembe plays soccer on a professional club team in New Mexico and with a team in his native Zimbabwe, and he also takes time to coach kids. This is what he tells them: Let yourself play freely. Let yourself play wholeheartedly. Let yourself have the grand old fun time you deserve to have, because that's the best thing you can do for your soccer.

Don't Be Afraid of Mistakes

To play soccer freely and wholeheartedly—and therefore to get into the zone and play your best—you must not let yourself worry about making mistakes. For one thing, worrying about them is counterproductive. For another, it's ridiculous, because there is no such thing as soccer without mistakes. Mistakes are part of the game, and they need to be part of your game plan.

People who don't know soccer very well often think the sport consists of an athlete taking the ball, dribbling the length of the field, and then cracking a shot into the goal. Of course these people are wrong. This happens so seldom as to be positively momentous. When the great Pelé did it, the goal was actually *named*. In 1961, in a game at Maracana Stadium in Brazil, he dribbled the ball from his own penalty area all the way to the other goal, beating six defenders and the goalie, and the goal he scored was named "Gol De Placa," which means "Commemorative Silver Plate Goal."[2]

But that was Pelé. You—and everybody else on the planet—will be dealing with a different reality. With every decision you make on a soccer field, you will be challenged. Your opponents will challenge you with all their speed and strength. The ball itself will challenge you, bouncing away erratically. Clumps of grass will trip you. Slicks of mud will pull you down. The teammate you expected to turn right will, without so much as mentioning it, suddenly turn left. You will take the most beautiful shot you have ever taken in your life, and the wind will lift it into the parking lot and drop it like a deadweight onto the hood of your father's car.

In fact, if you can count on anything taking place in a soccer game, you can count on mistakes taking place every three seconds; that's true in World Cup games, and it's true in the game you'll be playing next Saturday.

In soccer, there is no script, no magic formula. You don't automatically throw to first base or lunge for the quarterback or execute a back handspring on the second tumbling run. Instead, you play by making a million decisions, one after another, as the ever changing scene on the field unfolds. There is no way to predict what will happen at any moment, and no way to control it. There's no rule saying where you must kick the ball or to whom or when. To play the game well, you must feel free to make your choices and take your chances. You must play creatively and wholeheartedly. And you must never, ever hold back for fear of making mistakes.

"Here's the thing that sets this sport apart," said Thomas Rongen, the head coach of the New England Revolution. "The coach can't dictate what the players do. The players themselves have to be encouraged to solve the problems they encounter on the field. Even the youngest players must be creative. They must express themselves out there."

Rongen was speaking during a Revolution practice, in which Joe-Max

Moore and his teammates competed in a scrimmage so intense it seemed they might accidentally kill each other. Sweating and screaming, they held nothing back, colliding at full speed and tackling furiously. One of the players took a shot so potent the ball actually whistled through the air, and reporters on the sidelines had to throw themselves out of the way. It was an impressive shot (the reporters had to pick grass out of their teeth), but it missed the goal. Coach Rongen barely raised his eyebrows.

"The mistakes don't matter," he said. "Soccer players must explore. Therefore, they must be allowed to fail."

Play With Confidence

There is nothing more valuable to you as a soccer player, and nothing more important during a competitive game, than a feeling of confidence. When you feel confident in your ability, you feel powerful. You trust yourself to perform well, and you let yourself move freely. Your confidence helps put you in the zone in which you play your best; in this way, confidence is a self-fulfilling prophecy.

And if you don't have confidence, of course, you're sunk. You think about every little thing you're doing and whether you're doing it badly;

the radio in your head plays truly bad music at maximum volume. The worries make you tense and distracted and knock you out of the zone.

So you need to have confidence, in both your ability to make good tactical decisions on the field and in your ability to execute those decisions by handling the ball skillfully. And you acquire the confidence the way all athletes in all sports acquire it: You practice.

To learn wise tactics, simply play in as many soccer games as you possibly can. They don't need to be organized games or full-field games; two versus two in the driveway will work just fine. That's how kids all over the world learn to play smart soccer; they play constantly. By the time they've played enough games, they've figured out it's better to pass to an open teammate than to one who's covered, and it's better to step toward the ball than away from it, and it's better to be predictable on defense, and it's better to be unpredictable on offense, and so on and so forth.

In this country, however, most kids don't play soccer constantly in pickup games. Instead, they play on organized teams that practice twice a week and play games on the weekend. If this is your soccer schedule, you will indeed learn a lot, especially if you have a coach whose instructions you understand. But you also need to learn from experience. A coach cannot possibly tell you what to do in every single situation you'll encounter on a field, and a good coach wouldn't want to. The best way to learn the game is to play it, as much as you want, as often as you can.

As for ball skills, the way to learn them is simply to try them. Make sure you have the right size ball, because you won't learn properly with a ball that's too big. Then get your foot on that ball as much as possible, both at practice with your team and by yourself at home. Dribble the ball, juggle it, trip over it if you have to, but keep fooling around with it. Pass it against the garage wall, pop it up over the dog, maneuver it around the shrubbery until someone calls you in for dinner, and after dinner have your best friend bicycle over to play goalie so you can take shots. If you're feeling inspired, make your friend keep the helmet on.

Don't become impatient if, after just a couple of years, you can't dribble a soccer ball with both feet or trap it neatly or kick it far. These skills are tough to master! Just be sure that whenever you play, you have the opportunity to get your foot on the ball. In time, you'll become more and more skilled and confident.

Then, you'll need to reevaluate your ability. You'll need to figure out what you do well on a soccer field and what you don't do so well, and to focus your practice time on the weakest part of your game. If you can't trap the ball, practice trapping. If you always overshoot the goal, practice shooting. Any part of the game that you can fix, work on fixing.

It might seem obvious that you should do this, but lots of athletes—even elite athletes—ignore their weaker skills.

Julie Foudy, co-captain of the U.S. Women's National Team, was such a superb athlete and naturally gifted soccer player that she became a four-time Collegiate All-American and a member of the national team before she ever began to think about her weaknesses as a player. If she didn't play beautifully in a game, she simply vowed that she'd work hard at the next practice and do better next time, but she didn't focus during that next practice on anything specific. Then, in 1995 in the Women's World Cup, Julie and her teammates lost in the semifinal round, and Julie was devastated.

"That was the lowest depths of my career," she said. "Until then, I would never sit down and think, 'This is what I did well, and this is what

I didn't do well.' Maybe I was afraid if I worked on things I wasn't that good at, I'd lose my confidence. But no. If you work on things you aren't that good at, you get better."

During practice, work on the weakest part of your game.

Then you will feel so confident of your skills you won't worry about them or even think about them when you're playing. Your body will take over, to do the things you taught it to do in practice.

Think Only About Things You Can Control

When you play soccer, you are in charge of your effort, your enthusiasm, your sportsmanship, and your soccer skills.

You are *not*, however, in charge of the score. You are also not in charge of the referee, your coach's decisions, your parents' expectations, your opponents' ability, the weather, the condition of the field, or a hundred other things that exist independent of your attitude, thoughts, or actions.

Therefore, it is not useful for you to spend time thinking about those things or trying to control them. They distract you, and they take you out of the zone.

Imagine, for a moment, that you are in the stern of a canoe, and one of your teammates is in the bow, while your coach and parents watch from the shore. The current is swift, and you approach white water. What should you do?

Clearly, you can't try to stop the river. Clearly, you shouldn't clamber to the front of the canoe in order to manipulate your teammate's paddle. Also, it wouldn't be wise to jump overboard looking for help from the people on the riverbank. Finally, there's no sense wasting time contemplating whether or not you'll make it.

What you can do and must do is put your own paddle in the water and paddle like mad, and talk to your teammate so you're working together. That's the most you can do, and it's all you can do. If you make it through the rapids you'll feel proud of your efforts, and if you capsize, well, you'll be wet, but you will still have paddled hard, and you will still be exhilarated by your effort.

That's how to play soccer. You can't win your games by thinking about how much you want to win them. You can't win your games by thinking about how good or bad the other team is or how fair or unfair the referee or how proud or disappointed your coach or parents will be. You can't win your games by spending your energy on things that are out of your control.

Instead, you must think about what you can actually *do* to win your games, what is in your power to do, and then *do* it: practice your skills, play wholeheartedly, communicate with teammates, keep your spirits and energy up. In other words, put your very own paddle in the swift, wild water and take the ride. Play the game. Don't be distracted by the things you can't control, including the game's outcome. The playing is all that matters.

CHAPTER 3
GAME DAY

On game day, it's your time to have the best time—the exhilarating moments in the zone, the frustrating moments when you overshoot the goal, the tense moments when you're standing at the penalty line, the wacko moments when you collide with your teammate. All of these experiences are yours to keep, no matter who wins or loses the game, and as you grow older, you will remember them.

On game day, it's time to let yourself play freely. You've already done your practicing; there's nothing more that you can do to improve your ability. You can, though, prepare for the game, play it, and think about it afterward in a way that brings out the best in you as a soccer player.

Here's how you can play your very best on game day:

Before a big game in which it is especially important you play well, it's wise to take some time to review your strengths as a soccer player. If you always hustle, for example, or if you have good speed, or if you are a source of encouragement for your teammates, think about how important those things are for your team. Then be sure you use those skills as much as you can during the game.

Similarly, it is wise to think just a bit about your weaknesses and how you can keep them from having a big impact on the game. If, for example, you aren't a great dribbler, then remind yourself to pass the ball rather than to dribble a lot. If you tend to get emotional during the game, remind yourself that this doesn't help your team.

Finally, a good coach will have told your team only one or two very specific things to focus on during the game. You have probably been working on those things at practice, and the coach believes they'll help your team play its best. Before the game, then, review them. If your coach has a tendency to tell you six or eight things to think about, pick one or two of them that you need to remember most, and focus on them.

Appreciate Your Opponent

If you were asked to play soccer against a team of six-year-olds, you would have a very difficult time playing your best. If you played hard, you'd knock those little kids over and score at will.

After a while, you'd become bored, and you'd institute new rules so the game wouldn't be so lopsided. Your team couldn't score until it had completed ten passes, for example. Or you'd play with your eyes closed! Anything to make the game more interesting! As soon as you possibly could, you'd shoo the six-year-olds off your field so you could play hard and competitively.

The point is: You don't want to face an opponent who will not give you a challenge. You want to play an opponent who *will* challenge you, because only then can you play your best.

So try to look forward to meeting the opposing team on the field. Be careful not to exaggerate, or to dismiss, their ability ahead of time; don't imagine that because they are a strong team you are doomed to lose the game, or because they are a weak team you will surely win. Wait to see what they have to offer and respond by playing your game the way you play it best, freely and wholeheartedly.

Help Yourself Relax

It's normal to be nervous before a game and even good for your performance. If you are nervous because you are energetic and excited, the nerves probably feel like "butterflies," and they disappear once the action begins.

But sometimes you are nervous because you are thinking about those things you can't control. That nervous feeling doesn't go away when you play. Instead, it makes you tense.

Dr. Alan Goldberg, a sports psychology consultant in Amherst, Massachusetts, teaches this method for settling those "bad" nerves: Inhale slowly and deeply while you count to four; then exhale while you count to seven or eight. If you do this several times, it will help slow down your heart rate and shift your focus to your body and away from those things you can't control.

Dr. Goldberg teaches another technique that might work for you, too. Imagine a staircase that leads to a room. The staircase can go up or down; the room can be indoors or out. Then, fill that room with things that remind you of your successes. Put photographs in the room or posters of the athletes you admire or your athletic trophies and ribbons. You can be as imaginative as you want with your room: One young athlete imagined riding a dolphin down into the ocean and entering the room through sliding glass doors. So, make it a fabulous room, and every night for about five minutes before you go to sleep, visit that room in your mind. Then on game day, you can "visit" the room if you need to calm your nerves.

Use Visualization

No matter how much you practice, there will always be a soccer skill that you can't perform perfectly. If you find yourself worrying about that skill during a game, make sure you think specifically about how to perform that skill well.

For example, if you need to keep your knee over the ball when you shoot, think about keeping your knee over the ball when you shoot. Visualize it. Picture yourself putting your knee right over that ball and kicking it low and hard. *Do not* think about how you usually can't accomplish this, and *do not* visualize the ball flying up to the moon.

Does it take superhuman mind control to think about what should happen rather than about what shouldn't? No. It just takes practice. Practice thinking about what you *want* to have happen. Practice thinking about exactly what you should *do* to make it happen. Visualize it. During the game, when you must perform the skill, think those positive thoughts, or don't think anything at all.

Learn From Mistakes

As you know, you'll make mistakes in your games. The mistakes don't matter, but what you do afterward matters a great deal. You have several options.

One: You can throw yourself down and feel embarrassed or furious at yourself.
Two: You can keep yourself composed but still feel pretty bad.

Three: You can keep playing soccer wholeheartedly, because what possible good could it do for you to be depressed in the dirt or, for that matter, standing upright but feeling blue and diminished in strength and desire? Take an enormous guess.

Of course you chose number three, but it is much easier to choose that number from a list in a book than it is to actually pick yourself up after a gigantic mistake in a game and carry on wholeheartedly. In fact, you might find it practically impossible to do so; you might think it is against the laws of nature for a kid to, say, score a goal for the opponent and not feel like diving into the nearest storm drain.

But what if you could learn something from the mistake? What if you could put it to good use?

Dr. Hacker, the sports psychologist for the U.S. Women's National Team, teaches her athletes to go through a multi-step process when they make a mistake: They note what they have done; they replace the thought with thoughts about what they *might* have done; and then they move on.

Now, elite athletes are trained to go through this process even while the game is still going on. In fact, they go through it in the five or six seconds immediately following the mistake. Your best bet is to wait until the game is over and to go through the process more slowly, but you can still go through it.

Whenever you start thinking about a mistake you made—whether it's right after the game, or later that night, or even days later—simply take note in your mind of specifically what you did. Perhaps you scored against your own team by miskicking the ball off the side of your foot. Perhaps you moved in front of your own goalie. Fine. Note it. Then replace that thought with what you might have done. You might have kicked the ball with the laces of your shoe rather than the side of it. You might have listened to your goalie's voice more carefully. By replacing in your mind the image of the mistake with the image of a better play, you will have accomplished something useful for your soccer.

The next time you make a huge goof in a game, let it go. Keep playing. Just ignore it. Don't feel bad; that's useless. If you forget about the mistake entirely, fine. Forget it. But if the mistake starts to haunt you, if you find yourself thinking about it, go ahead and note it. Then replace it. You can do it.

You might think that sportsmanship is somehow separate from your efforts to play your best. You might think that when you are a good sport, you are being a nice person, but when you play well—and especially when you win—you are a successful athlete.

But that thinking is wrong. You cannot control the outcome of your games, so your success can't be measured by whether you win or lose.

You can, however, control your sportsmanship, and your success will indeed depend on whether you are a good sport or a bad one.

April Heinrichs was a star player at the University of North Carolina at Chapel Hill and the captain of the U.S. Women's National Team from 1985 to 1991. She is now head coach of both the University of Virginia's women's soccer team and the Under-16 Women's National Team. Many of her peers call her the best female soccer player ever.

"When you play soccer," she said, "you have to ask yourself questions that aren't only about skills and tactics but are about morals, too. Would you rather whack an opponent in the leg or get in a good defensive position to begin with? You have to take responsibility for yourself. The game will shed light on your character."

If you're reduced to tripping a kid as a last desperate attempt at defense, she says, your poor sportsmanship is really an indication that you weren't prepared for the game, or you were out of position on the play. In other words, you were *not* the best athlete you could be.

Similarly, when you don't muster the courage to congratulate an opponent, or when you talk back to the referee, or when you don't work hard because you aren't playing the position you want, you are failing to make the most of the things that are in your control. You are not putting forth your best effort. You are not the best athlete you can be.

After the Game

Immediately after the game, no matter the score, you need to behave beautifully. This takes courage whether you win or lose. You might be screaming with joy or fighting back tears, but at a certain moment, you will be asked to pull yourself together and shake hands with your opponent. Do it. If you are bursting inside with elation or with sadness, but you nevertheless stifle those emotions to shake hands, you are showing respect to your opponent and to the game.

Then, forget the game's outcome. Get an ice cream or a soda and enjoy the way you feel after you've worked hard.

At the right time—perhaps that evening, or a few days later— you can reflect on the game, on what happened and how you played. Think especially about what you did well. It's important to do this so you can control that radio in your mind should it begin to make sweeping generalizations such as "I always dribble out of bounds" or "I never make good plays." Don't let yourself get away with this sort of thinking. Instead, look at the truth of the matter. What did you do well? If you don't figure that out, you won't know the truth about your own abilities or what to focus on in practice.

If you also want to think about the mistakes you made, go ahead through the process of replacing an image of each mistake with an image of a better play.

And then, as soon as you are inspired to do so, get outside and play. Play as much as you want. Work as hard as you want. Don't do it for anybody else.

Do it for you.

It's important for you to take time to think a little bit about what it means to you to lose. If it means too much, you will have a very hard time becoming the best soccer player you can be. That potential outcome will be so important in your mind you won't be able to ignore it, so you won't be able to lose yourself in the zone.

So the sooner you make peace with the concept of losing, the better.

If you did all you could to prepare for a game you lost, and if you played with heart and spirit, you can have no regrets.

If you made mistakes in the game, you can go ahead and feel bad for as long as you need to, but as quickly as possible you should learn from them and move on.

If your teammates made mistakes, you can't blame them. You can give them affection and support so their spirits stay strong.

If you played beautifully, you should allow yourself to feel satisfied.

If your opponents played beautifully, you should appreciate their skill.

And if you find yourself thinking that you really, really, really, really want to *win* next time, put your paddle in the water. Get outside and practice. But remember: Winning may be your goal during a game or tournament or even a practice session, but it can't be the *reason* you play soccer. You play because it's fun to compete hard against an opponent. You play because it's fun to be with your friends on a team. You play because it's a blast to become so absorbed in a practice or game that you lose yourself in those moments in the zone. You play not for the winning but for the *playing*. Win—or lose.

CHALLENGING SITUATIONS

Sports psychologist Dr. Colleen Hacker was coaching a coed Under-11 youth team one day. As she began her halftime speech to her players, she noticed a boy from the opposing team sitting in her huddle. As gently as she could, she explained that he'd made a mistake.

"I know," the kid answered her. "But you guys have the oranges."

Dr. Hacker loves that story, because she loves that kid's attitude. She's sure he had no trouble during the game getting into the zone and playing his best. And if you are still younger than eleven years old, or if you are playing on a recreational team, you, too, may feel so lighthearted during halftime of your game that you're able to dive right into your opponents' oranges.

But the older you get, and the more competitive the team on which you play, the harder it will be for you to have such uncomplicated fun

CAN'T PLAY HERE, TODAY, COACH. THE FIELD IS THREE INCHES TOO WIDE AND FOUR INCHES TOO LONG, THE WIND IS GUSTING FROM THE WEST AT EIGHT MILES PER HOUR, THE FIELD SLOPES THREE DEGREES DOWNWARD AT ONE END, THE SUNBURN INDEX IS HIGH AND SO IS THE POLLEN COUNT...
BAROMETER
WEATHER

during your games. Soccer is an unpredictable game; problems crop up. Even when you're playing well and feeling good—even when you're in the zone—your team's fortunes can turn at any moment, and you can become distracted. Here are some problems that other kids have faced in game situations, and some solutions.

Bad Nerves

Before a big game, I'm so nervous I feel sick.

If your nerves feel a lot worse than just butterflies—if you have real stomachaches, for example, or you feel like throwing up—you need to figure out why you feel so bad about the upcoming game.

According to sports psychology consultant Dr. Alan Goldberg, you may simply be worrying about things you can't control, such as whether your team will win, or how good the opponent will be. If that's the case, you can change the focus of your attention by trying breathing and visualization exercises.

On the other hand, you may be feeling sick because you are simply dreading the upcoming game. You may not be looking forward to playing at all. In that case, you should ask yourself a few questions and try to answer them honestly. Do you really want to play soccer? Is it fun for you? If you can't answer yes, you need to take a break from the sport.

Your decision may disappoint your teammates or parents or coach, but you shouldn't continue to play, and you certainly won't play your best, if playing makes you feel sick. Perhaps after a season or two you'll feel the desire to play again. Great! You can always rejoin the game. You won't have wasted time. You will have saved your health.

Sometimes in the middle of the game, I have no idea what to do with the ball.

Indecision

Soccer can be a complicated game. With twenty-two players running around (plus the referee!) you might find it difficult to make a good decision in the heat of battle. That's why it's a good idea, whenever you can, to think about what you will do with the ball before it ever comes to you. If you think things out ahead of time, you will be able to act the instant you receive the ball, which will help the flow of the game.

Time itself is an element in every soccer game, though, and sometimes you receive the ball before you've had time to think of a plan. In that case, look for a teammate and pass. Soccer is a team sport, which is why you never have to be in a panic with the ball.

I get frustrated and lose my cool over a bad call by the referee.

You need to understand and remember that referees do not make bad calls because they favor one team. They make bad calls because, like you, they make mistakes.

How do you feel when you miskick the ball and it flies out of bounds? Would you like to hear a teammate yell at you for your mistake? Of course not. So treat the referee the way you'd want to be treated. Keep your cool and get on with the game. The sooner you become completely absorbed in the action, the better. Besides, the referee will most likely make a questionable call in your favor, and then you should feel that things are evened up.

Goal-keeping

I'm the goalkeeper, and whenever we lose I blame myself.

Keeping the ball out of the net is everyone's responsibility, and it is specifically the defenders' responsibility to keep the ball from getting to the goalkeeper and to make sure any shots that do get through are feeble and weak. So, it isn't fair to personally accept the blame for a loss.

On the other hand, if you made a mistake, such as letting the ball go through your legs or moving out of position, you can do what everyone else on your team does after a mistake: You can forget about it until the game is over and then review it in your mind, replacing the image of the mistake with the image of a better play.

Penalty Kicks

I can't handle the pressure of penalty kicks.

Some of the best players in the world struggle with penalty kicks. Here's one method for coping with the challenge. When you stand at the penalty spot, picture a teammate standing in the back of the goal, in the exact position where you would like your shot to end up. Then pass the ball, hard, to your imaginary teammate.

Bad Fields

I hate to play on a narrow field.

You are going to play soccer on a lot of different fields in your life, and you can't be too particular about how you handle them.

Yes, you may find it difficult to play the way you like on a narrow field, so think about how to solve that problem. When you play on a wide field, you see open space on the edges. But on a narrow field, you will have to look farther forward, toward the corner flags, to find the open space to play the ball. Think, and you'll solve your problem.

Bad Weather

I never play well in cold, wet weather.

If the weather is cold and wet for you, it's cold and wet for your opponents, too, and just as tough for them to play in. Take your mind away from that distraction and put your energy into solving the problem of a cold and wet field: Take shots from farther out, play more directly, and keep your heart rate up.

Trash Talk

When my opponents play dirty or talk trash, I feel like exploding.

What a great opportunity to look good! In contrast to a bunch of bullies, you can demonstrate some real class and play the game with dignity. To stoop to their level, to retaliate in words or with elbows, makes you look like a poor sport, too. So don't do it. Above all, don't let their behavior interrupt your ability to get into the zone of relaxed concentration. Focus. Play with composure, and speak only to your teammates.

The Scoreboard

In a big game, I can't help being constantly distracted by the score.

You know you can't play your best if you are distracted. You can't focus on the flow of the game if you're focusing on the scoreboard. So, first, you might need to remind yourself that the distraction is counterproductive and then try to become absorbed in the action.

If that doesn't work, you might need to figure out whether you are actually worried about the score, or whether, in fact, you are worried about what *other* people think of the score. Is your coach expecting a win? Are your parents hoping for one? It's great that these folks are interested in your team's success, and it's perfectly fine for them to pay attention to the scoreboard. You, on the other hand, have work to do. You can deal with their reaction to the score later, when the game is over.

If it's not a big game, I can't get excited about it.

Maybe you need to develop some perspective. Lots of kids all over the country and all over the world don't have an opportunity to play soccer. Maybe there's no league in their town, or they don't have money to join one, or they live too far from friends to have pickup games, or they can't play because they're too busy working.

They might be working cutting lawns. They might be working on a farm. They might be working in a mine. They might be stitching the soccer ball you're going to be playing with.

So take a moment simply to appreciate the opportunity you have to play the game. Then make the most of it.

CHAPTER 5

PLAYING WITH TEAMMATES

When Bobby Clark was young, he played soccer in Scotland and was one of the world's best goalkeepers. Now he is one of the world's best coaches. He has coached the Dartmouth College men's team and the New Zealand National Team, and he now coaches the men's team at Stanford University. He teaches soccer skills and tactics to his players, of course, but he also inspires them to create something bigger and better than each of them alone—a team. He cares about every one of the players, and they in turn care about each other. Their team feels like a family.

When you play soccer, you will have a wonderful time, and your team will play its best, if the team members feel like family and treat one another like brothers and sisters. If you work together toward a common goal—perhaps to have a winning season, perhaps to see every athlete on

the team improve, perhaps simply to spend time together playing—the journey toward the goal becomes its own reward. Then you have a winning season, no matter what your record.

To do your part to create harmony on your team, simply think of your teammates as brothers and sisters. Be *for* your teammates and not against them. Encourage them, support them, be kind to them, and remember always that you and they are in the game together.

Then, if you encounter these sorts of problems, try these solutions.

Weak Skill

I'm not as good as the other kids on my team, and I feel bad about it.

There's no reason to feel bad about your soccer ability. Work hard at practice and let yourself play wholeheartedly during games, and you will have an enormously positive impact on your team. It doesn't matter if you make mistakes, because all soccer players make mistakes; it doesn't even matter whether you're skilled with the ball. If you offer your best, your teammates will respond, and you will all benefit.

If your teammates don't seem to connect with you, or if they make you feel bad about your athletic ability, you need to talk to your coach. Explain how you feel, so your coach can help correct the problem. No team can thrive if the teammates don't treat each other like family, and your coach should be able to help your teammates appreciate you and rely on you.

If your teammates don't respond over time, you can consider playing for a different team. Of course you don't want to switch teams willy-nilly, but if you really feel you don't belong—if your teammates' ability is significantly different from your own and you can't find a way to contribute—you should find a team on which you'll fit more comfortably.

April Heinrichs, head coach of the University of Virginia's women's soccer team and the Under-16 Women's National Team, believes you will never reach your potential as a soccer player unless you play for teams on which you can thrive. You thrive when you are enjoying yourself. You thrive when you feel good about your teammates and they make you feel good about yourself.

Superstar

I'm the best kid on my team, and I'm frustrated.

If you are the best player on your team, you have a wonderful opportunity to make your teammates improve more quickly than they would without your skill to pull them along. If you think about your team rather than only about yourself, you can become a leader, and your teammates will not only learn from you and improve, they will admire you. How frustrating could that be?

Also, it's great to be the best player on a team, because you feel good about yourself, confident and proud. But in youth soccer, the best player on the team one year might not be the best the following year. A year is a very long time in a young person's life, and the changes that come in a year are enormous.

Short kids become tall kids, weak kids become strong, slow kids become fast, and uncoordinated kids develop coordination. So go ahead and enjoy your time as a leader and role model, but don't set yourself apart from your teammates. In time, the other kids may "catch up." You don't want their improvement to make you sad or jealous.

Defense

The goal scorers get all the credit, but I'm a defender, and no one notices my hard work.

You should celebrate your team's success, and that includes when goals are scored. So, give the goal scorers credit. But don't forget to celebrate the series of passes that led to the goal. And don't forget to celebrate the defensive play—perhaps your own—that gave your team possession of the ball in the first place. In other words, see the whole chess match, and appreciate everyone's hard work, not only when goals are scored, but on every play.

If your coach and teammates know soccer, they will do the same thing. If they really don't understand a defender's contribution to the game, have faith that they will in time. Meanwhile, take comfort in knowing that you, at least, understand the game in its complexity.

Cliques

Our team is broken into cliques. The starters stay with the starters, and we feel like second-class citizens on the bench.

It's hard enough to be on the bench; harder still when you feel no camaraderie with those kids who are starting. The situation needs to be fixed, and the good news is that you are in a position to help fix it.

First, you cannot consider yourself or your friends on the bench "second-class citizens." The starters are not better people than you are. They have a different role to play on the team just now, but that doesn't make them superior to you.

Brandi Chastain, a star forward on the U.S. Women's National Team, missed more than two years of soccer because of knee surgeries. During that time, she sat on the bench. It was a hard time for her, she says, but a valuable time, for she came to understand the enormous contribution that each substitute makes to a team.

Every player on your soccer team is unique and valuable. Each one of you is working to close the gap between your ability and your potential. And every one of you has an important job to do on the team. This is as true for you as it is for the starters.

So don't *you* think you are a second-class citizen, and don't act like one. You are a full-fledged member of the family. If you want to speak up, speak up. If you want to cheer, cheer. If you want to offer an opinion, offer it. If you want to reach out in friendship to one of the starters, reach out. You have just as much power as anybody else to pull the team together in friendship. Go for it.

My coach says my role on the team is to support the starters by practicing hard and being ready to play as a substitute. But I'm not satisfied with that.

It's one thing to play a supporting role, which can be crucially important to a team. It's another thing not to play.

A team works together, and every player has a role. If you are getting your fair share of playing time on a recreational team, but you don't like your role as a substitute, you need to remember that soccer is a team sport, and your contribution must match the team's needs.

On the other hand, if you play on a select team in which you aren't guaranteed playing time, and your role is, essentially, to spend nearly the entire game on the bench, you might want to switch to a less competitive team on which you can play. You'll never improve if you don't get to play. Most kids, by the way, would rather play a lot for a weaker team than sit on the bench of a stronger team.

COPING WITH COACHES

Every once in a while in your life, you will have the joy of playing sports for a coach who inspires and supports you. These people are special. They know the game of soccer, and they know how to motivate athletes.

They greet you when you arrive at practice and at your games.

They set goals for the season, so all the players on the team know what you will be working for together and what role each of you will play.

They understand how much you love to have fun with your teammates, and they participate in that spirit by bringing laughter as well as hard work to games and practices.

They remind you of your strengths, and they motivate you to work on improving your weaker skills.

They listen if you have a problem.

They do not criticize you, and they do not compare you to your teammates.

They challenge you by teaching you difficult new things, and they support you as you learn.

They help you become your best, and they help every one of your teammates become their best.

They are the leaders of the team, and you and your teammates follow with enthusiasm, desire, and trust.

Thomas Rongen, the head coach of the New England Revolution, said he has one criteria for evaluating youth soccer coaches. If a coach had twenty players on the team one year, and still has twenty players the next year, the coach has done a terrific job. The win-lose record is irrelevant. A successful coach connects with every single player in a meaningful way.

If you have such a coach, you are lucky. And chances are, at some time in your soccer career, you will have such a coach.

Chances are, though, that at some time during your career, you will have a problem with a coach, too. That happens in all sports, and soccer is no exception. A coach may not know soccer very well or may have favorites on the team or may overemphasize winning or may reveal poor sportsmanship. Because you are a child and the coach is an adult, you will surely wrestle with how to handle the situation. Here are some problems you may have, and some solutions.

Inexperienced Coaches

My coach doesn't know a lot about soccer.

In most youth leagues, soccer coaches are parents who volunteer their time to do something special—for you. It's very important that you recognize this and appreciate it. Now, you might not be accustomed to appreciating the things that adults do for you. You probably take it for granted when your parents clean up after you and drive you around and so on, but if you're old enough to begin playing serious soccer, you're old enough to begin appreciating it when people go out of their way for you, even if those people are your parents or other adults.

As for not knowing the game, your coach might, indeed, not know soccer well. Lots of parents who coach soccer have never played the game or studied coaching, and they often give you far too much instruction, too little time to actually play, and too much advice on game day. However, if your coach is supporting you and your teammates with encouragement, you will have a successful season anyway. Remember, you can always get the extra practice you need by playing pickup games with your friends. And as the season progresses, your coach will learn, too.

On the other hand, if your coach's lack of knowledge is causing you to feel bad about your efforts because the coach criticizes you or compares you to your teammates, then you probably aren't receiving any benefit from the experience. In that case, you might need to look around for another team.

My coach doesn't play me enough.

Fairness

If you're not playing, that's a problem. You should be playing, because you are entitled to the pleasure of the experience, and because only by playing will you improve.

The question is: Why aren't you playing? If your team is a recreational team and you are entitled to play at least half the game, ask the coach why you aren't getting your share of playing time, and if you feel awkward about asking, have your parents ask for you. Often, coaches are so busy they don't realize when someone hasn't played enough. Your mom or dad might offer to help keep track of who plays when, a task your coach will most likely be delighted to hand off.

If, on the other hand, you are on a select team in which you are not entitled to playing time, you need to ask your coach to tell you, honestly, why you aren't playing and which skills you should improve in order to play more. If you get the feeling you'll be on the bench even if you do improve, you will then have to decide whether or not to stay on that team. Then, remember: You can only become your best at the sport if you are thriving. Are you? Be honest with yourself. You may be better off in the long run playing a lot for a less competitive team, especially if you are younger than sixteen.

Yelling

The coach always yells at us when we make mistakes.
Unfortunately, a lot of coaches believe that by yelling, they are motivating their athletes to take mistakes seriously and therefore to make fewer of

them. Most of the time, though, athletes who are yelled at only become nervous about making more mistakes. Distracted by these worries, they can't get in the zone, and they don't play their best. This is probably happening to you.

Dean Conway, director of coaching for the Massachusetts Youth Soccer Association, says that a coach's yelling never makes players perform better; it is encouragement, not criticism, that makes an athlete play well, he says, and it is instruction, not criticism, that makes an athlete improve.

If you have a good relationship with your coach, you should explain how you feel. A good coach will listen to you, will understand that the screaming is counterproductive, and will stop.

If you don't have a good relationship with your coach, you should explain how you feel anyway. If the coach doesn't quit the yelling, you can find a new team.

Teaching Styles

I try to work hard, but I don't really learn a lot in practice.
Kids learn in different ways, and the way your coach teaches may not be the best way for you to learn. Some kids, for example, like to see things

demonstrated, while others prefer to hear things explained in words. Some kids learn quickly, while others learn slowly. Eric Wynalda, a star of the U.S. National Team, was diagnosed with dyslexia, a learning disability, when he was young and believes he had attention deficit disorder as well; many young soccer players have similar learning differences or disabilities.

So, it's a good idea to try to figure out how you learn. Do you like to think about what you are doing? Do you prefer to turn off your brain and simply try to imitate a physical movement? Can you always hear your coach? Can you see? Do you need to do things slowly? Do you like to do them again and again?

Ask your parents to help you define how you learn best. Then, tell your coach, or ask your parents to tell your coach, so you can receive the instruction you need. By helping your coach learn how to teach you, you will be creating a better coach.

Also, recent research shows that most people learn best if they learn only one thing at a time and have many hours to think about it before they're asked to learn something new.[3] Yet in order to make the most of practice time, many soccer coaches teach lots of skills at once. They are trying to do the best for their teams, and they may not be aware that this coaching method is counterproductive. In fact, the country's best high school and college soccer coaches never focus on more than one or two skills or ideas at each practice.

Positions

The coach plays me at the "wrong" position and I can't deal with it. All young players should have experience playing lots of positions and enjoying the different responsibilities that each requires. The best youth coaches will move players around so that everyone has the opportunity to score goals, defend, and play goalkeeper.

But when you get older, your coach will, indeed, put you in a position, and it may not be the one you want to play.

First of all, don't get mad at the coach. That's what coaches do; they see something in your ability and try to use it for the good of the team. Julie Shackford is a three-time collegiate All American soccer player who is now head coach of Princeton University's women's varsity team. When she was a young soccer player, she practiced constantly and developed what she calls "a great relationship" with the ball, which her coaches recognized and valued. They did not, however, think Julie was fast enough to play central midfielder, the position she desperately wanted to play.

"It took me a long time to know what position I was meant for," she said. "In fact, it wasn't until I was in high school that I finally knew where I needed to play. I said to the coach, 'Look, I may not be the fastest sprinter, but if you play me at center midfield, I'll make the fastest decisions.' I wasn't mad when the coach said no. But I kept at it. I was persistent."

Eventually, Julie won the position she wanted. But between the time she asked for it and the time she was allowed to play it, she kept playing in other positions, enthusiastically and wholeheartedly, and developing the ball skills that made her so valuable to the team.

You, too, may want to wait until you are in high school before you define yourself as a forward, midfielder, defender, or goalkeeper. And you, too, may have to wait to play the position you love. While you wait, tell your coach how you feel, keep working on your skills, and remember that the very best soccer players can play both offense and defense and can switch positions in order to do the most good for the team.

When the referee makes a bad call, our coach goes berserk.
Some coaches are too emotionally involved in the game, and there's not much you can do about it. Emotional coaches yell at the referees and at everybody else because they feel upset or angry or excited, and they haven't learned how to control themselves. If you play for such a coach, try to remember that the coach means no harm but is *not* a good role model.

Other coaches yell at the referee because they think by doing so, they are accomplishing something for the team. They think they are influencing the referee and also showing you, by their actions, how much they support the hard work you're doing on the field.

The very best high school, collegiate, and professional coaches, however, do *not* yell at the referee. Sometimes, if they think a referee has made an awful lot of mistakes, they will speak to the referee at halftime, but they know their words have very little influence, because the referees are simply calling what they see.

And the very best coaches also don't need to prove, by yelling at a referee, how much they support their players. The players feel supported by the coach's encouragement, advice, and attention.

CHAPTER 7

GUIDING MOM
AND DAD

If you are like most kids, you feel terrific when your parents can make it to your soccer games to watch you play. You're busy all day at school, and they're busy working at home or in an office, so it's hard for you to be the focus of their attention. Thus, it's special when they spend time at your games, watching you do your thing. It's also special to talk to them about your soccer experience, to hear stories about the sports they played when they were kids, and to go to them for advice when you need it.

But if you are like most kids, you don't want your parents to become *too* involved in your soccer career by taking over the role of a coach, or by setting goals for you.

Unfortunately, it's not always easy for parents to keep a balance between supporting you enough and involving themselves too much. Be-

cause they love you, they are trying to do what's best for you, and because you love them, you might not know how to ask them to change. Here are some problems some kids have had with their moms and dads, and some solutions.

Who Won?

My parents say that, above all, they want me to have fun when I play, but all they talk about after my games is the score.
Sports psychologist Alan Goldberg says that it's often difficult for adults to think about athletic competition without thinking about a game's score. In our country, he says, professional sports teams and professional athletes are always measured by whether they win or lose. The purpose of competition for these professionals is to determine a winner, so the skill (or even the extraordinary feats) of the loser are not celebrated.

Your parents, if they are sports fans, are accustomed to looking at sports this way. Thus, when you win a game, they might automatically want to congratulate you for a success, and if you lose, they might automatically want to console you.

You, however, have been absorbed in the *action* of your game. You haven't been concentrating on the results (which you couldn't control) but, instead, on the flow of the game itself. Thus, the score of the game might be far down the list of things that were important to you in the contest.

Go ahead and talk to your parents about what was important to *you* in the game. Above all, your parents want you to be happy and to feel good about your soccer experience, so they will probably be delighted to hear your thoughts.

Go to Practice!

My parents force me to go to soccer practice.

Why? Are they forcing you to go because you made a commitment by joining the team, and now they expect you to live up to that commitment? If so, they are trying to teach you a valuable lesson. When you make a commitment, you have to honor it—or leave the team—so your teammates don't have to deal with the suspense of whether you'll show up.

If, on the other hand, your parents force you to practice because they're trying to make you become a great soccer player, they are probably not going to succeed. No one can make you become your best except you.

Eric Wynalda, Brandi Chastain, Joe-Max Moore, Julie Foudy, and the many other elite athletes who offered advice for this book were all supported by their parents, who watched them play, drove them to games, hauled them to practices, laundered their uniforms, and kept dinner waiting for hours and hours. But none of these stars played or practiced soccer in order to obey or please their parents, and none of them relied on their parents to push them toward their goal of becoming their best.

Dad's the Coach

My dad is my coach. He always plays me, and I feel guilty.
You are not alone; most kids whose parents are coaches feel the same way. Talk to your dad away from the game and tell him how you feel. Tell him you want only as much playing time as you deserve. Then, trust that your dad will honor your request, and when he puts you in, play wholeheartedly, without guilt.

Complainers

My parents are always complaining to my coach about playing time, the field, my position, everything.

Parents are not coaches, and they must not interfere with coaching decisions. They should, however, stick up for you if they believe you are being treated unfairly, as long as they ask you first how you feel about things. Do you want more playing time? Are you playing a position you hate? It certainly cannot hurt, and it might indeed help, if your parents talk to your coach, in private, about how things are going for you. A good coach will either fix the problems or offer a satisfactory explanation for why they can't be fixed.

If your parents are complaining to your coach but you never asked them to and don't want them to, you need to tell them that you don't want them to interfere. Of course, it isn't easy to ask your parents to change their behavior in this situation or any other. But since they are doing what they are doing because they want the best for you, they will probably be happy to hear your views.

Before a game my parents give me a lot of specific coaching advice. How do I tell them to quit it?

Your parents are probably giving so much advice because they want you to play well. But before a game you need to be thinking only about the one or two things your coach has identified as important. If your parents give you lots of things to think about, too, you're going to feel confused by the conflicting advice and also distracted by the amount of information you're supposed to keep in your mind.

When your parents start to give you advice, you might ask them to give you information instead. Ask them, specifically, if they think you are ready for the game. Chances are they'll say, "Yes, you've practiced hard and you're ready." That's the best thing they can say, and the best thing you could possibly hear, before you hit the field.

In the middle of the game, I hear my dad calling out instructions. He was a great athlete when he was young. Should I obey?

Tommy Wilson, who played professional soccer for many years in Scotland, is now the football (soccer) development officer for the city of Glasgow,

Scotland. One year, when he was coaching a youth soccer team, he had a similar problem with one of the fathers.

"Every time this one boy got the ball, his father would shout, 'Do this, do that,' and the boy would say, 'I'm trying!' I spoke to the father at the end of one session, and he didn't agree with me that he should be quiet. But I said he had no choice. Six weeks later, the dad thanked me for the best advice he'd ever received. He said his son had finally learned the game, by making decisions for himself."

During a game, you need to lose yourself in the flow of the action. Also, you need to think for yourself. Obviously, you can't do either of those things if you're listening to instructions from your dad.

You might need to remind him that no one—not even a wonderful coach—can tell a soccer player what to do in the heat of the game.

Bad Advice

After a game, my parents sometimes tell me what I should have done differently. It's frustrating!

Ask your coach to organize a nice, long, full-field, competitive soccer game among the team parents. It won't take long for your mom and dad to realize how challenging the game is, and how you can't play well unless you allow yourself to make decisions spontaneously and wholeheartedly, even if they turn out to be mistakes.

Also, parents sometimes can't help offering you what they think is constructive criticism. It would be far better, though, if they told you what they thought you did well in the game. That's because you are probably quite aware of the mistakes you made, but less aware of the smart and successful plays. If you are to become your best, though, you need confidence, which comes when you give yourself credit where it's due.

I don't care that I didn't make a select team, but I think my parents are really disappointed.

Disappointments

Your parents may feel that by playing for a less competitive team, you will have a less rewarding soccer experience. They may have forgotten that in youth sports, no matter what team you are on, spectacular things can and do happen at any moment.

To remind your parents of this, you might want to ask them if they remember any athletic event from their childhood. Chances are they'll tell you stories in vivid detail. Perhaps your dad hit a home run one day in the neighborhood. Perhaps your mom won a relay race at camp. Sure, those events were not important to the world, or even to the world of sports. But they were sure important to your mom or dad.

Now it's your turn.

Injuries

My parents won't let me play just because my knees hurt a little bit.

You may have heard people say that if you want to become a success in sports, you have play in pain sometimes. But this is not true for young athletes. Unfortunately, it is true that elite collegiate and adult athletes frequently play in pain. Dr. Marjorie Shuer, a former intercollegiate swimming coach and assistant professor at Stanford University, says that superstars are often placed in a difficult position by coaching staff and teammates. If the injured athletes take time off to heal, they may lose their status in their sport and may be considered weak.

But young athletes accomplish nothing by playing in pain. When they do so, says Dr. Shuer, they jeopardize not only their athletic careers but their future active, healthy lives.

Your parents are wise to make you rest, and you were wise to tell them of your knee pain in the first place.

You should do the same thing next time you feel pain in any part of your body. Of course you'll feel winded if you run up and down the field. But an injury feels different, as you know. Don't cover up when you believe you are hurt, because the sooner you identify the trouble and start to heal, the better. Don't consider yourself a wimp for taking care of your body, and don't let anyone else make you feel that way, either. If you want to be your best, you must avoid a permanent or chronic injury. You do that by declining to play in pain.

CHAPTER 8

EASING YOUR DOUBTS AND FEARS

It's very sad but very true that kids drop out of organized youth sports all the time. According to one important poll, more than 75 percent of the boys and girls who play organized sports when they're six or seven years old drop out by the time they're fifteen.[4]

What a nightmare statistic! More than 75 percent dropping out! That's fifteen of the twenty kids on a youth soccer team! They quit the sport before they're even fully grown, so they never give themselves a chance to become as good as they can be. What's worse, when they drop out of organized soccer, they usually drop the game for good. In other countries in the world, the kids who don't make the school or town or select team can still play every day. But in the United States, where the game is still so new, most soccer is organized soccer. When kids drop out of the town league, their soccer days are usually over.

SOMETHING TELLS ME SOME OF THESE KIDS DON'T HAVE THEIR HEARTS IN THE GAME ...
COACH
OOF!
CRUNCH!
GNASH!
PICK!
56
12
6
13
27
4
17
16

Why do so many kids quit? There are lots of reasons, but mostly kids quit because they don't feel good about the game, and the game doesn't make them feel good about themselves. They have lost touch with the pleasure of playing for its own sake, and something else—worries about their ability, pressure to win, disappointment at not making a select team—takes the fun away.

Here are some problems that lots of young soccer players have faced in their soccer careers, and some solutions.

I'm Not a Great Athlete

I'm not very good at it, so I wonder if I should keep pursuing soccer.

You are young, and your athletic skills are just developing. Your body is still growing, and your thoughts and feelings about competitive sports are still evolving. You do not know yet if you will develop good skill with the ball, or the ability to read the game, or physical strength or mental strength, or the ability to lead a team, or any of the other skills—and there are so many—that make great soccer players.

So don't worry now about how naturally athletic you are. Practice your soccer skills, and then get out there and play. As long as you are enjoying yourself and playing a lot, your skills will improve, and you'll be doing the same thing the naturally talented athletes are doing—becoming your best. You cannot do anything more.

What does the future hold? Your best might turn out to be good enough to land you a place on an elite competitive team when you are older. That would be great. Or, your best may be good enough to land you a place on a less competitive recreational team. That would be great, too! Either way, you will have soccer in your life and the satisfaction of having reached your potential. Focus on reaching your potential and enjoying yourself, and your future will take care of itself.

I'm Burning Out

I'm playing soccer three seasons, and I'm losing my enthusiasm.
A lot of great athletes do not think it's a good idea to play three seasons. When you specialize so tightly in one sport, you really put yourself at risk of getting sick of it. Also, you don't get to play other sports. Why would

you deny yourself that? Why eat only chocolate ice cream? Have you never heard of mint chocolate chip?

On the other hand, you may feel pressure to play three seasons in order to increase your chances of making a select team. This is a real dilemma you must face, because, in fact, select teams are often made up of kids who play all the time and are well known to the selection committee.

You must ask yourself a question then. Is it better to take some time off and play wholeheartedly when you play? Or is it better to grit your teeth and play when you don't really want to in order to make a team on which you'll play even more? Is the future gain worth the present sacrifice? Is the future gain a gain at all? Won't you just burn out in a year or two?

The fact is, you won't play your best unless you are having fun, and you won't reach your potential unless *you* are the one who wants to practice and work hard. If you're sick of the sport, stop. When you feel the urge to play again, play. You will only become an elite player if the desire comes from you.

I didn't make the select team, and I don't feel much like playing the game.

When Eric Wynalda was a young kid, he tried out for the Under-14 district team in his home of Thousand Oaks, California. He didn't make it. He didn't make the Under-16 district team the next year, either, or the Under-18 team the year after that. Every time he was cut he was heartbroken, confused by the system of selection, and anxious to know what he was doing wrong.

He was forced to do a little soul searching, then, and to figure out why, if he wasn't good enough to play on the district team, he should keep playing at all.

But Eric did not quit. As long as there was a field outside with the sun shining down on it, and a soccer game to be played on it, he, for one, wasn't going to miss the action. He laced up his cleats and went out to play the game he loved.

Eventually, Eric did play on the district team, then the sectional team, then the regional team. Now he plays for Major League Soccer's San Jose Clash and for the U.S. Men's National Team. He is one of the best players in the world.

"When I got cut from that regional team year after year, it was the worst thing that happened to me and the best thing, too," he said. "I realized that the whole time it was happening I was still loving the game. And that's why I never stopped playing. It wasn't because I wanted to prove anything to anybody. I just loved this incredible game."

It was the *playing* of the sport he loves—not the winning of a particular game, or the playing on a particular team, but the *playing itself*—that gave him joy. Above all else, he loved the game, even when times were bad.

If you love the game, don't quit the game. You may need to rethink your goals and to play for a while on a less competitive team or in pickup games, but don't deny yourself the pleasure of playing soccer. Plus, as long as you keep playing, you will keep improving. Who knows what the future will bring.

We Keep Losing!

After a series of bad losses, I am dejected and lose my enthusiasm for the game.

Soccer is a funny game because the best team sometimes loses. You have surely seen games in which one team outshoots the other by 24–3 and loses the game 3–0. That's soccer. So, keep your perspective. Even more importantly, you must remember that after a loss, you should feel okay if, nonetheless, you were prepared for the game and you played as well as you could. The same holds true for a series of losses.

Also, in youth leagues, most kids play in a division for two years and often stay with the same group of teammates. The first year, when they are the youngest kids in their division, they lose a lot of their games; the second year, when they are the oldest kids, they win most of them. A year makes a huge difference in a child's development, and if this is your year to lose, be patient. Your time should come.

Finally, you have to learn how to lose in sports. Sometimes after a loss you really won't care that much. Sometimes you'll be devastated. After a series of losses, you might really feel like quitting the game. That's when your character will show through. That's when you'll learn something about yourself. Your goal must be to exhibit courage and grace when times are bad, and to keep your enthusiasm and faith in yourself.

CHAPTER 9

YOUR TIME IS NOW

Mike Burns, a midfielder for the U.S. Men's National Team and for Major League Soccer's New England Revolution, has played soccer in stadiums all over the country and the world. He has played in the Olympics, and he has played in the World Cup, but he will never forget the title game of the Marlboro, Massachusetts, Youth Soccer League, a game he played when he was fourteen years old.

In the second half, with the score tied 2–2 and just seconds left on the clock, Burnsie took a shot and scored and was instantly tackled in a frenzy of joy by his teammates. They just mobbed him. That goal was as much fun for him as the goals he scores now with literally millions of people watching and cheering. The thrill never changes. It is a thrill when you're ten just as it is when you're twenty.

And it's not only goal scoring that you experience fully when you're young. You experience the fury and frustration of losing, the euphoria of the opening whistle, the friendships with your teammates, and, best of all, you experience the zone, in which you lose track of time and find in its place every single molecule of a moment in the game.

You feel all of these things during your youth soccer games just as intensely as you will ever feel them in your life. This is true whether you're on a town team or a select team, it's true whether you're a substitute or a starter, it's true whether you win the game or lose it.

Yes, you will be more skilled at soccer when you are older. The game will be faster and more complex. But the great joy of the game never changes. You will experience next Saturday's game with all the emotion, all the heart and soul, of a collegiate or an Olympic or a World Cup athlete.

You may be just a kid, but you are not pretending to be a soccer player.

You are the real thing.

And your time is now.

NOTES

[1] W. Timothy Gallwey, *The Inner Game of Tennis*, (New York: Random House, 1974), p 13.

[2] Michael LaBlanc and Richard Henshaw, eds., *The World Encyclopedia of Soccer* (Detroit: Visible Ink Press, 1984), p. 86.

[3] "Time Called Key Factor in Learning Physical Skill," San Francisco Chronicle, August 8, 1997, p. A6.

[4] Wolff, Rick, *Good Sports*, 2nd ed. (Champaign, Ill: Sagamore Publishing, 1997), p. 21.

INTERVIEWS

Thank you to the following coaches, athletes, doctors, and sport psychologists who granted me personal interviews.

Mike Burns—midfielder, U.S. Men's National Team; captain, New England Revolution (MLS)

Brandi Chastain—forward, U.S. Women's National Team; assistant coach, women's varsity soccer, Santa Clara University

Bobby Clark—coach, men's varsity soccer, Stanford University; youth soccer coach

Jamie Clark—defender, men's varsity team, Stanford University; youth soccer coach

Tommy Clark—midfielder, Albuquerque Guekos, Albuquerque, New Mexico (USISL); youth soccer coach

Dean Conway—director of coaching, Massachusetts Youth Soccer Association; youth soccer coach

John Doyle—defender, San Jose Clash (MLS)

Ronni Fair—defender, U.S. Women's National Team; defender, women's varsity soccer team, Stanford University; youth soccer coach

Julie Foudy—midfielder, co-captain, U.S. Women's National Team

Dr. Alan Goldberg—sports psychology consultant, Competitive Advantage, Amherst, Massachusetts

Fred Grainger—interim coach, men's varsity soccer, Phillips Academy, Andover, Massachusetts

Dr. Colleen Hacker—sports psychologist, U.S. Women's National Soccer Team

Dr. Stuart Hauser—director, Judge Baker Children's Center, Boston, Massachusetts

April Heinrichs—coach, women's varsity soccer, University of Virginia; head coach, U.S. Women's Under-16 National Team

John Kerr, Jr.—midfielder, New England Revolution (MLS)

Steve Locker—coach, men's varsity soccer, Harvard University

Joe-Max Moore—midfielder, U.S. Men's National Team; New England Revolution (MLS)

Cailin Mullins—assistant coach, women's varsity soccer, Stanford University; youth soccer coach

Alberto Naveda—midfielder, New England Revolution (MLS)

Methembe Ndlovu—midfielder, Albuquerque Geckos, Albuquerque, New Mexico (USISL); Highlanders FC Zimbabwe; youth soccer coach

Andy Nelson—coach, women's varsity soccer, Wellesley College

Fran O'Leary—coach, men's varsity soccer, Dartmouth College

Thomas Rongen—head coach, New England Revolution (MLS)

A.J. Sauer—forward, men's varsity soccer, Stanford University; youth soccer coach

Bill Scott—coach, men's varsity soccer, Phillips Academy, Andover; youth soccer coach

Julie Shackford—coach, women's varsity soccer, Princeton University; youth soccer coach

Dr. Marjorie Shuer—assistant professor in human biology, Stanford University

Dr. Daniel Snyder—orthopedic surgeon, Boston, Massachusetts

Steve Swanson—coach, women's varsity soccer, Stanford University; youth soccer coach

Scott Turco—goalie, men's varsity soccer team, Harvard University

Tommy Wilson—football development officer, Scottish Football Association, Glasgow, Scotland; youth soccer coach

Kevin Wylie—defender, New England Revolution (MLS)

Eric Wynalda—forward, U.S. Men's National Team; San Jose Clash (MLS)

BIBLIO-GRAPHY

Bridges, Lisa J., and Eugene Wong. "A Model of Motivational Orientation for Youth Sports: Some Preliminary Work." *Adolescence*, Vol. 30, No. 118, Summer 1995, p. 437.

Chalip, Laurence, and B. Christine Green. "Enduring Involvement in Youth Soccer: The Socialization of Parent and Child." *Journal of Leisure Research*, Vol. 29, No. 1, Winter 1997, p. 61.

Gallwey, W. Timothy. *The Inner Game of Tennis*. New York: Random House, 1977.

Hellmich, Nanci. "Few Kids Get Daily Exercise." *USA Today*, July 1, 1997, p. D1.

Hoch, David, and Michael Klausner. "The Elements of Team Chemistry." *Soccer Journal*, Vol. 42, No. 3, May/June 1997, pp. 37–38.

LaBlanc, Michael, and Richard Henshaw, eds. *The World Encyclopedia of Soccer.* Detroit: Visible Ink Press, 1994.

Lief, Fred. "Foul Play: How Grown-Ups Ruin Kids' Sports." *Parents Magazine*, Vol. 71, No. 4, April 1996, p. 48.

Orlick, Terry. *In Pursuit of Excellence.* 2nd ed. Champaign, Ill.: Leisure Press, 1990.

Pollack, Robert. *Soccer for Juniors.* New York: Charles Scribner's Sons, 1980.

Razzi, Elizabeth. "Did Child Labor Make That Toy?" *Kiplinger's Personal Finance Magazine*, Vol. 50, No. 12, p. 46.

Robinson, Andy. "The Will to Win: A Comparative Study Between Intercollegiate Athletes and Pre-adolescent Soccer Players."M.S. in Ed. Diss., University of Kansas, 1996.

Soccer Jr. Coaches' Edition, Triplepoint, Inc., 1997.

Swoap, Robert A. "Sport Psychology Issues in Youth Soccer." *The U.S. Soccer Sports Medicine Book.* Baltimore, Maryland: William E. Garrett, Jr., Williams & Wilkins, 1996.

Tutko, Thomas, and Umberto Tosi. *Sports Psyching.* Los Angeles: J. P. Tarcher, Inc., 1976.

Wolff, Rick. *Good Sports.* New York: Dell Publishing, 1993.

Woods, Karl M. *The Sports Success Book.* Austin, Tex.: Copperfield Press, 1985.

Youth Soccer. The American Orthopaedic Society for Sports Medicine.

INDEX